CRE▲TIVE
HOMEOWNER®

DESIGN IDEAS FOR
decks

CREATIVE HOMEOWNER®, Upper Saddle River, New Jersey

CREATIVE
HOMEOWNER®

A Division of Federal Marketing Corp.
Upper Saddle River, NJ

VP, Editorial Director: Timothy O. Bakke
Production Manager: Kimberly H. Vivas

Senior Editor: Fran J. Donegan
Assistant Editor/Photo Researcher: Sharon Ranftle
Assistant Editor: Jennifer Ramcke
Editorial Intern: Amy Knych

Senior Designer: Glee Barre
Cover Photography: John Parsekian
Cover Design: Glee Barre
Back Cover Photography: *(top left)* Brian Vanden Brink, architects: Elliot & Elliot; *(top right)* Brian Vanden Brink, architect: Rob Whitten; *(bottom left)* John Parsekian; *(bottom right)* Melabee Miller, builder: Doyle Builders
Indexer: Schroeder Indexing Services

Current Printing (last digit)
10 9 8 7 6 5 4 3

Manufactured in the United States of America

Design Ideas for Decks
Library of Congress Control Number: 2003108701
ISBN: 1-58011-147-5

CREATIVE HOMEOWNER®
A Division of Federal Marketing Corp.
24 Park Way
Upper Saddle River, NJ 07458
www.creativehomeowner.com

SAFETY

Though all the designs and methods in this book have been reviewed for safety, it is not possible to overstate the importance of using the safest possible construction methods. What follows are reminders—some do's and don'ts of work procedures and tool safety that apply to deck building and home projects in general. They are not substitutes for your own common sense.

- Always use caution, care, and good judgment when following the instructions and procedures described in this book.

- Always be sure that the electrical setup is safe, that no circuit is overloaded, and that all power tools and outlets are properly grounded. Do not use power tools in wet locations.

- Always read container labels on paints, solvents, and other products; provide ventilation; and observe all other warnings.

- Always read the manufacturer's instructions for using a tool, especially the warnings.

- Use hold-downs and push sticks whenever possible when working on a table saw. Avoid working short pieces if you can.

- Always remove the key from any drill chuck (portable or press) before starting the drill.

- Always pay deliberate attention to how a tool works so that you can avoid being injured.

- Always know the limitations of your tools. Do not try to force them to do what they were not designed to do.

- Always make sure that any adjustment is locked before proceeding. For example, always check the rip fence on a table saw or the bevel adjustment on a portable saw before starting to work.

- Always clamp small pieces to a stable work surface when working on them with a power tool.

- Always wear the appropriate rubber or work gloves when handling chemicals, moving or stacking lumber, or doing heavy construction.

- Always wear a disposable face mask when you create dust by sawing or sanding. Use a special filtering respirator when working with toxic substances and solvents.

- Always wear eye protection, especially when using power tools or striking metal on metal or concrete; a chip can fly off, for example, when chiseling concrete.

- Never work while wearing loose clothing, hanging hair, open cuffs, or jewelry.

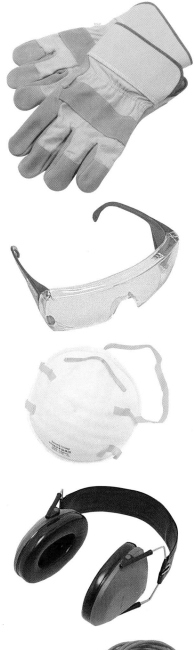

- Always be aware that there is seldom enough time for your body's reflexes to save you from injury from a power tool in a dangerous situation; everything happens too fast. Be alert!

- Always keep your hands away from the business ends of blades, cutters, and bits.

- Always hold a circular saw firmly, usually with one hand on the trigger handle and the other on the secondary support handle.

- Always use a drill with an auxiliary handle to control the torque when large-size bits are used.

- Always check your local building codes when planning new construction. The codes are intended to protect public safety and should be observed to the letter.

- Never work with power tools when you are tired or under the influence of alcohol or drugs.

- Never cut tiny pieces of wood or pipe using a power saw. Always cut small pieces off larger pieces that are securely clamped or fastened to a stable work surface.

- Never change a saw blade, drill bit, or router bit unless the tool's power cord is unplugged. Do not depend on the switch being off; you might accidentally hit it.

- Never work in insufficient lighting.

- Never work with dull tools. Have them sharpened, or learn how to sharpen them yourself.

- Never use a power tool on a workpiece—large or small—that is not firmly supported.

- Never saw a workpiece that spans a large distance between horses without close support on each side of the cut; the piece can bend, close on and jam the blade, and cause saw kickback.

- Never support a workpiece from underneath with your leg or other part of your body when sawing or drilling.

- Never carry sharp or pointed tools, such as utility knives, awls, or chisels, in your pocket. If you want to carry such tools, use a special-purpose tool belt with leather pockets and holders.

contents

There are many good reasons for adding a deck to your home. With a deck, you expand your living space and increase your home's value for a tiny fraction of what it would cost to build an addition. And you expand your living style as well. A deck pulls you and your family away from the TV and out into the fresh air, where friends feel more inclined to chat and family members enjoy each other's company more easily than when they are cooped up inside the house.

Decks are simple structures to design, but there are some pitfalls to avoid. Many first-time designers neglect

to consider the way that the deck relates to the yard and how it complements the style of the house. Some homeowners forget that the deck will be used for a range of outdoor activities and develop a design that is either too large or too small, or does not include the amenities they need. Or they neglect the weather conditions and build a deck in an uncomfortable environment. This book will help you avoid these problems, and it provides photographic ideas that are both attractive and functional. You will learn to think in terms of the needs of your family and to work within the limitations of your property and budget.

FAR LEFT A curving deck provides the owners with a great view of the beach and the sunrise.

LEFT The use of planters and furniture helps create activity areas on the deck.

ABOVE Open spaces provide room for a number of different deck activities.

design guide

T here are two things every designer needs: inspiration and the design expertise to turn vague ideas into concrete plans. This chapter is a good starting point for acquiring those skills. You'll find plenty of inspiration through dozens of photos of well-designed decks as well as ideas that you can simply "borrow" for your own use. You'll also find an easy-to-follow guide to help you come up with ideas on your own. Thinking about the activities you and your family enjoy the most will get you started on creating your dream deck.

LEFT Curves, built-in seating, and distinctive decking patterns help create a unique overall deck design.

RIGHT Personal tastes play a big part in the design of your deck, but make sure unusual ideas, such as the design of this railing, meet code.

BELOW The designers of this deck based its shape on the shape of the house. This small deck can be reached from two rooms in the house.

OPPOSITE Curves add interest to the design. The curved railing softens the part of the deck that juts out into the yard.

beginning your design

Many people are reluctant to make design decisions because they don't think of themselves as designers. But if you take the time to think things through carefully and enlist the opinions of others, you may be pleasantly surprised at the ideas you generate. You have memories of pleasant places you have enjoyed, as well as dreams of the ideal place to relax. Of course, dreams can rarely be re-created in the real world. But by letting your imagination run loose and tapping into those images, you can provide yourself with a font of design concepts that will help you come up with a down-to-earth deck design.

Begin by imagining your ideal deck, and ask family members to do the same. Think about its design, accessories, and any special elements you would like your deck to contain. Keep track of your ideas by drawing a series of rough sketches as you proceed. Expect to fill a wastebasket or two with these. Don't think of them as actual designs so much as focal points for conversations—it's sometimes easier to point to a place on your drawing than to walk around the house.

TAKE ADVANTAGE OF FREE IDEAS

Feel free to steal ideas from other people. (The best architects do not hesitate to do so.) When you see a deck that particularly pleases you and seems appropriate for your situation, take a few photos and jot down some notes. Talk to the owners about how their deck works for them. Most people will be flattered that you like their deck and will be more than glad to talk to you about it. You will not only learn about pleasing designs and materials, but you can avoid the mistakes they made.

You will probably come up with an idea that you later discard, because you either no longer like the way it looks or discover that it will not be practical. Don't be discouraged. In fact, expect it to happen, and happen several times, before you come up with the design that best suits you and your family.

uses for your new deck

Call a family meeting to discuss your deck plans. Find out everyone's vision of the deck. What would they like it to look like? Where would they like it to be? The backyard is the logical choice, but an enlarged front porch may better suit your needs. Or it may make more sense to design a deck that wraps around two sides of your house. How large a deck do you want? If a large deck would cut into your yard area, making it tough to play croquet, or if it would throw shade on the flower bed, you may want to scale back your plans. But if you rarely use your yard or hate maintaining the lawn, a larger deck will make gardening chores easier. Most importantly at this point, consider the activities that will take place on the deck. Then take a walk together around your property, examining possible sites. Think about how a deck could enhance the way you now use your yard. Consider new ways to enjoy outdoor living as well. The following pages present some things to think about.

LEFT Even tiny decks can serve an important purpose. This area is part of a larger structure, but imagine having this view outside of your home and not being able to enjoy it.

ABOVE Decks are great gathering places and often the center of entertaining. The curved portion creates a natural conversation area.

RIGHT The desire for a deck often leads to other things. Spas require beefed up structural support.

COOKING AND ENTERTAINING

Entertainment is high on many people's list. Plan for a cooking area as well as a place for a good-sized table for seating smaller groups or for buffet settings if you have large parties. For nighttime entertaining, think about installing a lighting scheme.

Locate the grilling area as far as possible from other use areas so that you won't have to worry about kids bumping into a hot barbecue. Leave ample room for cooking "assistants" so that friends can gather around and talk as you turn the steaks. You may want to build a complete cooking center with counter space, cabinets, and even an outlet for a small refrigerator.

Make your deck easy to get to. The more entrances, the better. Wide doorways—sliders and French doors are good—will make it easy to flow from house to deck. Large windows that look onto your deck will entice people outside. If you plan to do a lot of eating on your deck, make sure it's close to the kitchen. If you can open a window and hand food out to people on the deck, so much the better.

Consider what the walkways to and from your deck will be like. Will people have to skirt around furniture to get there? Will the kids be tracking dirt on a living room carpet? Will there be a bottleneck during a party? Coming off the deck into your yard, will you want some sort of patio surface to ease wear and tear on the grass and gardens?

ABOVE Here's a deck built for entertaining. The spa is great for small groups, and the dining and conversation areas in the background can host larger gatherings.

LEFT Dining areas usually depend on the type of furniture that you have. Be sure to plan enough room to accommodate foot traffic and someone pushing back from the table.

LIGHTING. If you tend to eat and entertain after dark, consider your deck's lighting. A motion-sensing flood-light provides security and lights your way as you bring in groceries, but it makes for an unappealing dining ambiance. Subtle, low-voltage fixtures set into steps or posts provide a better solution for dining and entertaining on the deck. Most lighting plans call for a combination of both types of lighting.

Installing line-voltage lights—the type of lighting used inside the house—will require burying the lines in waterproof conduit and installation by a licensed electrician. The alternative is low-voltage light, which operates on just 12 volts rather than the 120 volts of standard line voltage.

In addition to placing low-voltage lights in steps and posts, consider lining a path that leads up to the deck with small lights. When choosing these fixtures, be sure to select fixtures that are attractive during the day as well as at night. You may also want to consider using lights for decorative effect. For example, you can install low-voltage lights in the garden to highlight plantings that are visible from the deck. In-ground fixtures cast their light upward, creating interesting areas of shadow and light on trees and shrubs. Many fixtures have lenses that let you aim the light beam.

Avoid installing too many lights. With low-voltage layouts, a few well-placed lights is more dramatic than the glare produced by too many lights.

TOP RIGHT A line of lights flanking a path that leads to the deck is a welcoming sight.

RIGHT Step lights, especially on a long flight of stairs such as these, provide safe passage for those using the deck.

BELOW Light means safety, but a good lighting plan contributes greatly to the overall look of the deck.

design guide

RIGHT Conversation areas like this one are appealing when they are protected from the late afternoon sun. The dimensions of this deck contribute to the cozy feeling.

OPPOSITE TOP Place the new deck to take advantage of the path of the sun during different times of the year. Don't forget to include the view in your plans.

OPPOSITE BOTTOM Conversation and just plain lounging around usually require a combination of sunlight and cooling shade. When planning, consider the shade cast by nearby trees.

A PLACE TO RELAX

Consider what your future deck will be like during all the seasons when you are likely to use it. Pay particular attention to sun and wind patterns.

SUN. Decide how much sun and how much shade you want, and take this into account when siting your deck. If you live in the northern hemisphere, a north-facing space will be in shade most of the day. This can be an advantage if you live in a very hot climate and a disadvantage for most everyone else. An eastern exposure gives the deck morning sun and afternoon shade; this is often the best choice in warm climates. In cold climates a southwest exposure usually provides full and late afternoon sun.

WIND. Take note of wind patterns on your property. If heat is a problem and you want to enjoy a breeze, or if the site is too windy, it may be possible to create a solution by changing the landscaping. Try pruning or adding plants.

OPPOSITE Mature trees and shrubs can help you create a backyard sanctuary from the world.

LEFT Make high fences open and airy. They will provide privacy without making the yard appear smaller.

BELOW A deck built high in the trees has privacy and great views.

PRIVATE SPACES

Decks are often raised off the ground, which might mean you and your family will be on display for all the neighborhood to see. Existing fences may be too low to shield you from view. Sometimes the problem can be solved by stepping the deck down in stages. In most settings, decks work best when built low to the ground. If your entry door occupies a high position, you'll find it best to build a landing and stairs or a series of tiers leading down to a low-built main deck.

You may have to take direct action to achieve privacy. You don't have to build an unfriendly, solid wall to avoid the feeling you are being watched. If you feel overexposed, a well-placed trellis provides the base for some nice climbing plants to look at and creates a pleasant enclosure. Another solution is to plant border trees and shrubs.

Fences are another option. There are many styles and materials from which to choose. High solid fences provide the most privacy, but an imposing design isn't very friendly, and it can make your yard seem closed in and smaller than it really is. Soften fences by using them as a backdrop for plantings.

design guide

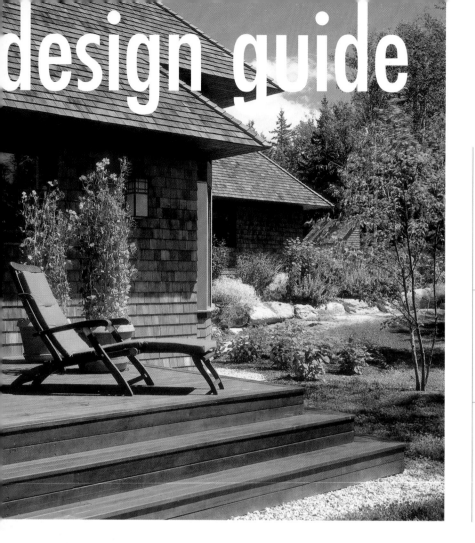

LEFT A deck built low to the ground may be all you need to maintain your privacy from the neighbors. A deck that places you above border plantings and fences will put you on display.

RIGHT Separate areas on the same deck also create privacy. In this case, a chance for family members to get away from one another.

BELOW A large, heavily wooded property affords its own type of privacy. It also gives you a chance to include elements such as the clever bridge.

Family members need some privacy among themselves as well. By building with different levels, including a conversation pit, or even by just letting the deck ramble a bit, you can create areas that are separate but not walled off. Careful placement of activity areas can also help create private sections. For example, if you are installing a spa or a cooking center—areas that tend to draw a crowd—place private areas on the other side of the deck.

Think about whether you want your deck to feel airy and open to the world or cozy and secluded. These effects can be achieved in many ways. A small deck will feel cozier than a large deck. Low benches and railings designed with large open spaces in them give an open feeling. A deck that hugs the house will have a more sequestered feel than one that juts out into the yard.

In addition, consider the foliage that will surround the deck both now and later. As that nearby tree grows and spreads, your deck will feel more solitary. Hedges can provide the same enclosure as railings, whereas surrounding your deck with low-growing plants will leave it permanently exposed to the surroundings.

design guide

SMART TIP

ENJOYING THE VIEW

Plan your landscape along with your deck to maximize your viewing pleasure. Orient the deck so that you will be looking at the best features of your yard. If possible, plan your landscaping along with the deck to enhance this pleasure. Foliage of any kind sets off the natural tones of the wood. Think about the flowers, shrubs, climbing vines, and even trees that you might want to place near the deck. Locate bird feeders, trellises, or a small pool where they will achieve the best effect.

CONTAINER GARDENING. It is almost impossible to put too much foliage on or near a deck. And just about anything that can be grown in your yard can be grown in containers. Find planters that will complement the design and architecture of your deck and house, or plan to build some from the same material as your decking. With small movable planters you can move flowers around as they come into season. With enough sun, tomatoes, peppers, and all sorts of vegetables do well. An herb garden flourishes without a lot of work and still looks great after a bit of harvesting. The avid gardener may consider putting cold frames or a greenhouse on or next to the deck.

ABOVE In some cases, the view itself becomes part of the overall deck design.

LEFT The design of this deck incorporated the mature shade tree shown to the right.

RIGHT A landscaped slope, complete with pond, occupies one corner of this deck.

design guide

A PLACE FOR CHILDREN TO PLAY

The idea here is not to build a jungle gym into your deck but to provide an inviting place where kids can play. If small children will use the deck, select your materials accordingly. Hard-edged toys can damage cedar or redwood in a hurry. Treated fir or pine will hold up better, but you'll need to seal it with a penetrating finish to protect it from the elements.

A deck can also make it easier to keep an eye on the kids. If this is a concern, design the deck so that you can watch them easily from inside the house. That means the deck should be off the kitchen or family room.

RAILING RULES. If the deck is more than a foot or two off the ground, you'll have to make sure any railings are childproof. Use vertical balusters spaced 4 inches on center. Do not install ladder-type railings that are easy to climb. If you're in doubt, check with the local building department. Even if the deck you're planning will be below the height at which the code requires a railing, you should still consider installing a sturdy railing if you have young children. The railing will act as a fence to keep them safe and will also prevent them from wandering off.

Remember to inspect decks that are used as play areas often for splinters and raised fasteners.

RIGHT If you have children, be sure to select a railing design and deck material with them in mind. Talk with a contractor about natural materials and new engineered products.

BELOW Ground-level decks and high railings are great for keeping kids safe, but nothing compares with adult supervision. Place the deck so that it is in view from inside of the house.

INCLUDING A POOL OR SPA

As long as you use rot-resistant lumber, wood makes an ideal surface next to a pool or whirlpool spa. It's softer than tile or concrete and is slightly absorbent, making it a pleasant place to sit or lounge after going for a swim. An inexpensive aboveground pool gains a lot of class when you surround it with a deck. But compare your options carefully. A deck built around the typical aboveground pool is usually 4 feet off of the ground, making for a very bulky object in the middle of your yard. From an aesthetic standpoint, it may make more sense to install an in-ground pool with a ground-level deck.

If you are putting in a whirlpool spa or hot tub, position it for privacy as well as an unobstructed view of the stars. Install comfortable seating areas around it and perhaps an overhead structure for shade, and remember to allow a convenient, inconspicuous place to stow the cover while using the spa.

ABOVE FAR LEFT A sunken spa turns this corner into a private retreat.

ABOVE NEAR LEFT Redwood remains cool to the touch longer than masonry patios.

LEFT Engineered wood products provide long-wearing and attractive poolside surfaces.

BELOW This decking connects the pool with the design of the house.

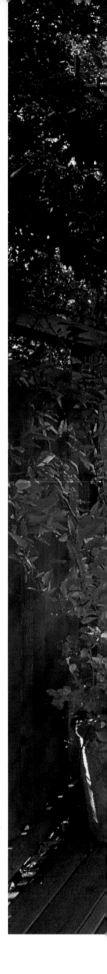

Adeck usually does not stand alone; it is attached to your house and plays an important part in the overall landscape of your yard. So always consider not only how the deck itself will look but also how it will fit in with its surroundings. This does not always mean striving to make the deck blend in; it is after all a different sort of structure than the house. But the contrasts should be pleasing rather than jarring.

Think of the deck as being part house and part yard. A well-designed deck should blend the two, balancing the amenities of the household and the yard.

RIGHT Think of your new deck as the focal point of your yard. Here the deck is built around a pool and hot tub.

BELOW The graceful curves in this deck and railing soften the line of the house to which it is attached.

making a visual statement

SMART TIP

DECK DESIGN SOFTWARE Programs you can run on your home computer or laptop can help you organize your design ideas. Produced by a number of companies, the software makes simple work of drawing decks, railings, planters, and other deck amenities. Some versions show your work in three-dimensional rotating images that allow you to make a virtual tour of the deck and the surrounding area. The programs can also provide materials lists and building instructions.

design guide

THE MOST VISIBLE ELEMENTS

Something to keep in mind: although the decking will be the greatest amount of material you install, it will not be the most visible element from most perspectives. Railings, stairways, and fascia boards are often the things people will see first. If the deck is raised very high, the posts and understructure may become the most prominent visual elements.

In this book, you'll see a number of railing and bench designs. You can either choose from these, create your own, or combine the features of two or more designs.

If your deck needs a skirt, choose this element carefully as well. Latticework makes a good choice, but a solid skirt can be made to mimic the siding on your house, which helps to visually tie the two structures together.

LEFT A distinctive railing design is often the first thing a visitor will notice on a deck.

ABOVE Overhead structures, such as arbors, will command attention on your new deck.

BELOW If part of the deck is visible from above, use the opportunity to install decking boards in a custom pattern.

ABOVE LEFT This substantial railing system is counterbalanced by the narrow deck and screened porch.

ABOVE RIGHT A lack of built-ins and a simple curving shape work well with the clean lines of this house.

LEFT This railing lightens the overall mass of the deck, but be sure the design meets code in your area.

BASIC DESIGN ELEMENTS

Though you probably do not want your deck to completely blend in with your house, you do not want it to be jarringly different, either. Elements to consider when seeking to match your deck with your house and yard are mass, shape, and color.

MASS. A large deck will overpower a small house, making it appear even smaller than it is. Decide which vantage points are the most important: how will your deck appear from where people are most likely to look at it?

A deck's visual mass is not just a function of its actual size. Building low to the ground or designing railings that are low or light-looking will help the deck recede and thus appear smaller. Large visible beams, railings that are densely packed with boards, and wide fascia boards all will make a deck seem more massive. If your deck must be raised 10 feet or more above the ground, you will have to use bulky 6x6 posts. (Actually, the higher you go with these, the less thick they appear.) You may be able to cover these with landings or deck sections that are more airy.

You can make the house to which the deck is attached appear less massive by planting trees or tall shrubs next to it. A long exterior wall with plenty of windows and doors will appear smaller than one with large, unrelieved expanses of siding.

To increase a deck's area without making it look too big for the house, design it to hug the house rather than jut out into the yard. You might consider even wrapping the deck around a corner or two. This will make the deck appear to be a more integral part of the house rather than a stand-alone structure.

SHAPE. The shape you choose for your deck should harmonize with the lines of your house. First, consider the general orientation. The alignment of a deck should in most cases be much more horizontal than vertical. This will give it the light, breezy feeling that you want from an informal space. However, if you are building a raised deck, there will necessarily be up-and-down lines. If your house is tall and narrow, some of this vertical sense will be welcome, and you may want to repeat these lines.

Second, think in terms of overall shape. If your house has a pleasing L-shape, for example, you can repeat that with a deck. A house with a confusing shape can be softened with a deck that is simple; a plain-looking house can be jazzed up by a boldly shaped deck.

Most people choose to have a deck that is attached to the back of the house. However, you may want to consider other options, such as the Japanese-style engawa, which wraps around the house, a deck that incorporates a tree, an island deck, or a peninsula deck.

DECK SHAPE OPTIONS

WRAPAROUND

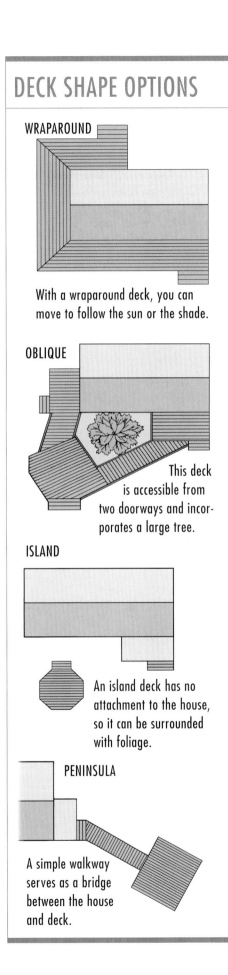

With a wraparound deck, you can move to follow the sun or the shade.

OBLIQUE

This deck is accessible from two doorways and incorporates a large tree.

ISLAND

An island deck has no attachment to the house, so it can be surrounded with foliage.

PENINSULA

A simple walkway serves as a bridge between the house and deck.

OPPOSITE The many angles of this sitting area help define its intended use.

RIGHT Curves help soften the hard lines of many houses. They also tend to blend better with the deck's natural surroundings.

BELOW This design provides natural spaces for built-in seating and an interesting decking pattern.

design guide

LEFT White railings matched with dark decking is a classic and elegant combination.

RIGHT Decks left to weather naturally must be treated periodically with a preservative sealer.

BELOW A light-color stain complements the siding on this beach house.

COLOR. In most cases, people choose either to stain a deck to a redwood or cedar color or to let the wood turn grey over several years. These are good choices for the deck itself, because they project a relaxed, casual mood. And when many people think of a deck, they automatically think of exposed natural wood. But if your deck will abut a formal portion of your house or if the usual decking colors simply will not go with your house, do not hesitate to consider applying a semi-transparent or solid, opaque stain. There are two advantages to this course of action: you will get the color and look you want, and one that goes with your house; and the pigments in the stain can help protect the wood from the sun's damaging ultraviolet rays.

theme and variation

As you look at other decks, you will encounter many design ideas that appeal to you. Strive for a sense of unity in your design rather than incorporating a bit of everything. The best decks take one or two ideas and then work out variations on those themes.

The idea could be a gently curved line; if you have a large octagonal-shaped projection, you may be able to add a smaller version of it elsewhere on the deck; or you can build a table or a bench with the same shape. Remember that often the most visible elements of a deck are those that project vertically. Choose your railings or benches to harmonize with the overall structure. Planters can take on shapes that mirror the deck structure.

A great deck will have a stunning focal point, something that immediately grabs the attention of everyone who enters. Perhaps you already have one—a beautiful tree, a lovely view, a nice pool. Or you can supply the eye-catcher yourself—a hot tub, a huge potted plant, or a series of flower boxes.

ABOVE The rustic theme of this deck matches the style of the house as well as the surrounding wooded area.

RIGHT Repeating a detail helps create a sense of harmony in the design. Notice the arches along the underside of the covered area. The colors selected for the decking and the roof structure work well together.

solving problems gracefully

While you are dreaming up visions of beauty, don't ignore the nitty-gritty problems, both large and small, that will come up. The idea is to make lemonade out of lemons, to turn knotty conundrums into pleasing points of interest. Now is the best time to start thinking about them.

* Storage can be dealt with by providing access to the area under your deck, by building an attached shed, or by using interior space that has been freed up by the deck. List the things you need to store and make sure you have room for them, or they will clutter up your deck.

* Drainage will usually only be a problem in the future if it is a problem now. For minor problems, you may need to plan for a gravel-filled trench in the ground to collect runoff from your deck. If you have major problems, be sure to deal with them before you build. A sloping site will make building more difficult but also presents an opportunity for an interesting multi-leveled deck.

* Trees on a deck site also present a chance to do something stunning. Find out how quickly your tree will grow, and plan to leave ample space.

* Overhead protection, if you do not have the foliage on your site to do the trick, can be achieved with some very nice louvered structures, or pergolas, or with brightly colored awnings. For areas with heavy rainfall, you can build an extension of your house's roof.

ABOVE A slight elevation separates the main deck from the pool area.

LEFT A wall of built-in planters adds a practical use to this long, narrow deck.

ABOVE RIGHT A painted pattern is an eye-catching detail.

RIGHT A bridge made of decking materials becomes a focal point.

special features for decks

LEFT For much of the day, the open design of a pergola-like shade structure protects inhabitants from the direct rays of the sun by providing a dappled shade pattern.

OPPOSITE The design of this structure is reinforced by the fan pattern of the deck boards. Together they create an area that is separate from the rest of the deck.

FAR RIGHT BOTTOM Even small decks can accommodate an overhead shade structure. Here the designer used one to create a small sitting area that is out of the flow of the deck traffic that moves between the stairs and the French doors.

NEAR RIGHT Classic columns rather than typical decking materials are used to support this pergola. The large white columns work well with the light-colored decking materials and house siding.

special features for decks

ABOVE Rather than place this gazebo on the main part of the deck, the designer chose to build an extension to the structure. It is a separate area, but it ties to the main section through the use of similar materials.

RIGHT Large decks require variations in design approaches to avoid looking boring. Here, the sweeping curve adds interest, as does the vertical structure set in the corner. Notice how the curve in the gable echoes the curve of the deck railing.

LEFT Lighting can increase the time you spend on your deck. Be sure to provide safety lighting around steps and paths.

RIGHT A lattice-like railing adds distinction and a sense of enclosure to this shady deck.

BELOW LEFT When planning your deck, think in terms of modules to handle different activities.

creating private retreats

SMART TIP

CREATING SHADE There are many structures that can provide shade for your deck. But sometimes it is best to place the deck under mature trees. You get relief from the heat, and much of the landscaping is already in place.

special features for decks

ABOVE This gazebo-type structure not only provides shade and a separate seating area, it also adds architectural interest to the deck and the home to which it is attached.

RIGHT This open structure provides an airy destination for this deck. This type of design element will become the focal point of the deck, so choose materials and components that work with the overall design.

LEFT A simple traditional gazebo, such as this, adds a touch of elegance to the deck. The vaulted exposed-rafter design helps make the structure seem less confining than a solid ceiling would.

BELOW The slatted walls of this structure provide protection from low-angle sun without sacrificing ventilation. The owners chose to keep the main part of the deck and the structure separate from one another.

LEFT There is no reason to reduce the number of plantings you want near your deck because you are including hard structural elements in the design. This filigree structure serves as a base for climbing plants and hanging containers.

planters and

LEFT Built-in planters act as anchors for your deck landscaping. Here they are used with container plants.

BELOW LEFT Benches not only make the deck more convenient, they also act as a boundary on ground-level decks.

ABOVE RIGHT The designer of this deck combined seating and planting space. Be sure to plan planter location with the plant's welfare in mind.

RIGHT Built-ins serve as planters, seating, and in this case, a colorful border that runs the length of the deck.

benches

SMART PLANNING TIP

BUILT-IN PLANTERS and the plants that they hold add color and texture to your deck. When designing planters, pick the plants first and then build planters that best accommodate their growing habits.

LEFT The seat of a built-in bench should be about 18 in. from the surface of the deck for maximum comfort.

RIGHT Place planters near stairs, as shown here, to create a welcoming entry point for your deck.

BELOW Although not as common as built-in planters and benches, water features add a unique soothing element to your deck design.

LEFT Place built-in seating where it will do the most good. Here the designer surrounded the spa with benches, eliminating the need for deck furniture.

ABOVE Filling planters with colorful annuals allows you to change the look of the deck throughout the outdoor season.

RIGHT MIDDLE One solution to dealing with a mature tree where you want your deck to be is to frame the new deck around it.

RIGHT BOTTOM Ledges built around the tops of planters add a nice architectural touch, and if sturdy enough, make plant maintenance easier.

original railings

ABOVE You can't buy this railing as a prefabricated unit—or even duplicate it exactly. That's why custom designs can add a touch of distinction to your deck.

RIGHT The designer of this deck used an undulating railing-and-deck design to build around the large tree.

FAR RIGHT TOP A shingle-covered low wall, rather than a traditional railing with balusters, works well in this rustic beach setting.

FAR RIGHT BOTTOM This deck and railing take their cues from the house. Notice how the railing follows the line of the overhang and complements the house trim.

lighting

LEFT Post lights illuminate the path between different areas of the deck while step lights built into the risers add a measure of safety to the deck.

RIGHT Lights and a screened area combine to make the deck usable at night. When bugs aren't a problem, fixtures mounted on the gable light up the rest of the deck.

BELOW The openness of this home's design allows interior lights to illuminate parts of the deck. When selecting outdoor lights, avoid installing too many fixtures and placing them where they will create glare for people using the deck.

ground-level decks

Many people believe that only raised decks are truly dramatic. But ground-level decks, including those that are a step or two up from the yard, offer their own design advantages. They are easier to build than their high-flying counterparts, and they tend to blend easier with the size and shape of the house. They also have more direct contact with the surrounding yard. That means it is a simple matter to make the yard, gardens, walkways, and deck part of one integrated design. On a practical note, these decks rarely require railings.

LEFT A curving deck that surrounds this family-room addition adds to the family's usable livng area.

decks that ease their way into the yard

SMART TIP

BROAD LANDINGS Create wide steps of different sizes as a transition to the yard. They offer more design possibilities than standard-size stairs, and they can serve as platforms for container plants or other objects. An added bonus: because there is no railing, there is nothing to interfere with any views you may enjoy while sitting on the deck.

ABOVE Container plants and hanging baskets create a movable landscape for this deck.

LEFT A simple change of direction in one corner breaks up the monotony of this rectangular deck.

ABOVE This simple ground-level deck seems to complete rather than compete with the design of the shingled house.

LEFT The white railing and painted brick supporting the deck tie this structure to the siding on the house.

RIGHT A perimeter of washed river rock gives the impression that the deck is floating in place. The rock also separates the deck from the rest of the yard.

BELOW An intimate deck fits nicely with the overall design of the house.

BELOW RIGHT Steps that flare out at the bottom tie this deck directly to the surrounding yard.

RIGHT A sloping yard often means that some of the underside of the deck will be exposed. Here, solid skirting solves the problem and enhances the design.

FAR RIGHT A few things contribute to the cozy feeling of this deck, including the numerous plants and the use of the fire pit as a focal point.

BELOW A low-profile design that fits with the mass of the house, a lack of railings, and the use of natural materials make this deck seem like part of the rugged surroundings rather than an intruder.

SMART TIP

DECK ACCESS The door that connects your house to your deck, or at least its location, may be just as important as the design of the deck itself. Decks that are easy to get to are used more often than decks that are a struggle to reach. Family rooms, great rooms, and kitchens offer the best access points. Decks located off of these rooms are truly outdoor living spaces. Decks off of bedrooms tend to be private retreats rather than spaces that the whole family can enjoy.

LEFT This small deck receives a design boost thanks to the angled stairs.

RIGHT Let the shape and style of your home suggest a location and style for your deck. This deck fits nicely in the L shape; the two levels separate activity areas without overpowering the house.

MIDDLE LEFT Lush foliage at its base seems to give an airy, floating appearance to this deck.

BELOW LEFT A small open space that is detached from the rest of the house provides the ideal setting for this intimate deck.

ABOVE The fence at the far end of this deck serves two purposes: it provides privacy from the neighbors, and it serves as a wind screen on stormy days.

LEFT This is truly a ground-level deck, and it appears to blend into the yard. On a practical note, choose materials rated for contact with the ground for this type of design.

RIGHT Nothing beats an overhead arbor for providing dappled shade. Note how one side of the deck is completely fenced in. This type of design provides protection from the late afternoon sun.

BOTTOM RIGHT Simple built-in benches provide extra seating for this covered deck without obstructing views of the surrounding area.

LEFT A number of details make this deck special. Note the curved benches, the curved step leading up to the spa, and the built-in planters. The wide second-step deck boards form a herringbone pattern that seem to point down to a slate tile patio.

RIGHT Brick pavers are a favorite patio material because they are attractive and easy to install. Notice how the bench on the patio ties the deck and patio areas together.

BOTTOM Even a simple deck design is enhanced by the addition of the adjoining brick paver patio.

decks paired with patios

ground-level decks

LEFT Although small, this deck is full of interesting details. The angled covered corner is perfect for a picnic table. The roof overhang and the tree provide shade. The half-round-shaped steps and spindle-like skirting add design interest.

RIGHT A ground-level deck usually does not require a railing, but this simple design enhances the look of the deck.

BOTTOM RIGHT Here's a simple, clean design that does not disturb the peaceful setting. A ground-level design and the use of similar materials on the house, porch, and deck help the deck blend in with its surroundings.

raised decks

The most obvious reason for wanting a raised deck is that the view is better from up there. But sometimes the slope of a yard or the design of a house makes anything but a raised deck impractical. The owners of houses with walk-out basements usually find that a raised deck is the only practical way to gain access to the deck from a main living area, such as a family room, great room, or kitchen.

Raised decks also provide the answer to those homeowners who want the luxury of a deck located off of a second-floor bedroom.

LEFT Views are important, but a raised deck should have a logical connection to the rest of the house.

raised decks

LEFT Lattice panels screen out the area beneath a raised deck while providing adequate ventilation. Here, airy lattice complements the mass of the other decking materials.

RIGHT Walk-out basements call for an open design, like this one under the deck. Be sure to include under-deck lighting to illuminate the area at night.

BELOW AND RIGHT The design ideas did not stop at deck level here. The designer created a simple lattice pattern to decorate the top of the posts on this deck.

SMART TIP

LATTICE IS OFTEN USED to hide the exposed underside of a raised deck. If lattice is in your plans, be sure to include a door to give you access to the area beneath the deck for storage. If the deck is high enough and there is a doorway to the house nearby, keep the underside open and turn it into a patio.

raised decks

soaring above it all

ABOVE Even views as spectacular as this one seem more dramatic when viewed outdoors from a deck. The diagonal bracing shown above gives this deck a cantilevered appearance.

ABOVE Convert what would otherwise be an unused flat roof into a functional raised deck. Here, the cantilevered balcony adds interest as well as square footage.

RIGHT To provide deck access, a gable window opening was enlarged to accommodate a door that leads to this raised deck.

BELOW LEFT Standard house framing can usually support the weight of a rooftop deck, but check with the local building department to be certain.

ABOVE RIGHT Planning a deck that is accessible from second-floor rooms actually provides you with two outdoor living areas—and one comes with overhead protection.

BELOW FAR RIGHT This deck follows the front facade of the house, including a jog outward that follows the contours of a family room.

NEAR RIGHT Match the style of the deck to the house. Note the log-style railing and the siding.

SMART TIP

TALK WITH THE BUILDING INSPECTOR before planning a deck for a difficult building site. Many houses that require a raised deck are often located on isolated, sloping building lots that sometimes require extra-strong framing to support the deck. This is always true of building sites where the deck overhangs a steep hill. Your first step in such a situation is to check with the local building department for any special code restrictions. In many cases, the deck contractor will need to drill down to bedrock to set the support posts. You may find it necessary to have your deck contractor consult with a structural engineer to help design the deck's support structure.

The building inspector can also alert you to any zoning regulations that may pertain to your deck. Many municipalities have setback requirements to which any new structure you add to your property must adhere. Some areas even restrict the size of your deck, limiting the total square footage. All areas have requirements for railings and stairs. In most places, railings must be at least 36 inches high, but for decks built high off the ground, 42 inches may be the code-approved height.

LEFT Raised decks often provide great views, so don't obstruct the scenery with a solid railing. There are many other options possible, including railings with clear panels and the type of railing shown here. (Check with your local building inspector for code-approved railing designs.)

LEFT Although you will want to consider views when planning your new deck, don't forget to consider the amount of shade and sunlight that the area receives, as well as the direction and strength of the prevailing winds.

BELOW Curved built-in seating adds a distinctive feature to this deck. It also serves as a safety railing.

raised decks

LEFT Using the same decking and railing design in both the front and back of the house can tie the two areas together. Here, a narrow side deck reinforces the connection.

RIGHT Out on the deck, the stunning views command attention, but from inside the house, the deck itself is part of the view.

RIGHT The surrounding area can help set the ambiance for your deck. Here, the nearby vegetation makes the deck appear as if it is floating on the tree tops.

BELOW All decking materials are made to stand up to normal conditions, but some locations, such as this waterside deck, require materials that are specially treated for severe conditions.

raised decks

LEFT If there is enough room available, plan on installing switchback stairs with landings for a raised deck. They will increase the cost of the project, but they are easier to climb, and their complex lines tend to enhance the overall look of the deck.

RIGHT The shape of the house often dictates the location and overall design of the deck. This raised deck fits nicely into the corner of this L-shaped building. The color choice helps the structure blend in with the rest of the house.

BELOW LEFT Even a small space can be made appealing. Here, there is just enough room for a sitting area that commands views of the surrounding woods. The area also acts as an inviting entry into the house.

BELOW RIGHT A level change increases the design options of most raised decks. A step or two up or down creates an entirely new activity area. The designer of this deck emphasized the change by adding the small shade structure.

chapter five multi-level decks

Creating a multilevel deck design provides the ultimate in flexibility, especially if you will be building on a sloping site. A series of levels that step down from the house can follow the contour of the yard, creating a pleasing design. But consider a multilevel deck for a flat yard as well. Your overall design will be visually interesting, even if only a step or two separates the levels from one another. The different levels provide natural settings for different deck activities, such as cooking, dining, conversation, and relaxing.

LEFT A complex multilevel design works best when attached to a large, ornate building such as this.

LEFT The gradual stepping down of these levels softens the transition between the formal house and casual boat slip.

RIGHT A sloping building site offers the perfect opportunity for a multilevel deck design. Here the levels seem to cascade down the side of the hill.

BELOW The designer of this deck turned an out-of-the-way corner into a focal point. The raised level makes it easier to accommodate the built-in spa.

create a variety of vantage points

multilevel decks

ABOVE By following the contour of the hillside, this deck blends in with the surrounding area—an important consideration when trying to preserve the natural beauty of a remote building site.

RIGHT This cabin in the woods calls for a simple deck design. Although difficult to see here, there is a single step down to the area with the two chairs. Simple cutouts accommodate the two trees near the porch.

OPPOSITE Distinctive railing and arbor designs help draw attention to the small raised sitting area on this deck. The raised area also has a herringbone decking pattern to further distinguish it from the rest of the deck.

SMART PLANNING TIP

CONNECTIONS BETWEEN LEVELS For an open plan, use wide steps between levels. For a cozier ambiance, use narrow stairs with railings or built-ins on the higher levels.

ABOVE Colorful throw cushions turn the wide steps shown here into additional seating. For safety, place cushions on the bottom steps and keep them away from high traffic lanes, such as areas in front of doors.

RIGHT Relate the size and shape of your deck to the structure to which it is attached. A deck of this size that is all one level would be too imposing; the use of levels helps soften the impact without sacrificing square footage.

LEFT Here's an example of how a small yard and a relatively small deck can benefit from the variety offered by a multilevel design.

multilevel decks

LEFT The use of similar materials makes the porch another level in this multilevel deck design.

RIGHT This rambling deck follows the contours of the property and fits well with the design of the house. The levels fall away from the house to the area used for relaxing in the foreground.

BELOW FAR LEFT A gazebo placed in the corner of a deck will become a destination on its own. Here, that quality is enhanced because the structure is raised above the rest of the deck.

BELOW LEFT The steps along the side of the house continue the design theme begun by the raised level in the background.

chapter six multi-function decks

F

ew decks are used for just one purpose. The trick is to plan for multiple uses before construction begins so that everyone is happy with the results. But don't go overboard. Unless you have unlimited space and budget, trying to cram too many ideas into one design will lead to disaster. You won't be happy with the results, and you will be way over budget. Start by planning for the one or two major activities that you and your family plan on enjoying on your deck, and work out from there. Here are some ideas to get you started.

LEFT Here's a full-service deck design incorporating a spa, dining area, and inviting conversation pit.

create

TOP LEFT Try to tie the different activity areas of your deck together. Notice the built-in table for serving food and drinks just off of the circular conversation area. The overhead structures provide needed shade to two areas of the deck.

RIGHT The owners of this deck designed a cooking and serving area for those times when they entertain. The lower counter comes in handy for serving. Improve outdoor cooking areas by including electrical service and a small refrigerator.

BOTTOM LEFT Decks need not have complex designs to be great for entertaining. The area in front of this pool house is welcoming and inviting.

areas for entertaining

plan space for a soothing soak

LEFT The platform surrounding this spa provides seating and a space for people to lie down and sunbathe. Place your spa so that equipment hatches are accessible for repairs and maintenance. It is also a good idea to keep the spa out of high-traffic areas.

TOP RIGHT This spa is paired with a unique fountain to complete this deck. If installing a spa on a deck, be aware that you will need to drain the spa periodically and should make arrangements to remove the extra water.

MIDDLE RIGHT Before ordering the spa, check with your deck builder to make sure that the structure can handle the weight of a spa filled with water and people. In many cases, you will place the spa on a concrete pad that is installed on the ground and then build the deck even with the top of the spa.

BOTTOM RIGHT The owners of this yard used decking materials to build a walkway off of the main deck to the spa located in the corner of the yard.

multifunction decks

some other popular uses

LEFT Adding a screened structure to your deck will allow you to use the deck during bug season. A wooded location would be unbearable on a warm summer evening without some protection.

ABOVE A lot of thought went into designing this corner. Here, the deck provides the background for a koi pond and seating area. Notice how the bench faces the deck rather than the view.

BELOW Indulge your hobbies on your new deck. This design features a potting bench located out of the way under the arbor. The structure is useful for hanging plants.

multifunction decks

SMART TIP

DEFINE AREAS A level change is the most obvious way to define areas, but there are other less drastic ways. Use built-in benches or planters as boundaries; movable planters and furniture can also define areas.

LEFT A deck should relate to the yard as well as the house to which it is attached. The stairs and bridge connect the sophisticated design of this deck with the surrounding natural spaces. Viewed from this side of the stream, they serve to draw the eye toward the deck and the house.

ABOVE One way that people who live in areas with cold winters can enjoy their deck for most of the year is to include a sunspace in their design plans.

RIGHT Adding personal items will individualize the design of your deck. An old potting bench, cut flowers, and candles complete the overall look of this deck.

resource guide

The following list of manufacturers and associations is meant to be a general guide to additional industry and product-related sources. It is not intended as a listing of products and manufacturers represented by the photographs in this book.

APA-The Engineered Wood Association

(APA) *is a nonprofit trade association, the U.S. and Canadian members of which produce a variety of engineered wood products. Its primary functions include quality inspection and product promotion.*

P.O. Box 11700

Tacoma, WA 98411

Phone: 253-565-6600

www.apawood.org

Arch Wood Protection *manufactures preservatives and additives to enhance the properties of wood. Its products are used in the treatment of Wolmanized Natural Select wood, among other products.*

1955 Lake Park Dr., Suite 250

Smyrna, GA 30080

Phone: 770-801-6600

www.wolmanizedwood.com

California Redwood Association, *a nonprofit trade association, offers extensive technical information about redwood, including grade distinctions, structural applications, and finishing characteristics.*

405 Enfrente Dr., Suite 200

Novato, CA 94949

Phone: 888-225-7339

www.calredwood.org

CorrectDeck *offers durable, sturdy composite decking made from recovered Maine hardwood and polypropylene. It has regional offices across the country.*

Correct Building Products

15 Morin St.

Biddeford, ME 04005

Phone: 888-290-1235

www.correctdeck.com

Elyria Fence Inc. *provides custom decks, fences, trellises, and arbors all year round. Its Web site has a photo gallery of its many styles and designs.*

230 Oberlin-Elyria Rd.

Elyria, OH 44035

Phone: 800-779-7581

www.elyriafence.com

The Flood Company *is a 150-year-old, family-owned corporation that makes a variety of paint-related products, including penetrating stains, sealers, wood renewers, and cleaners. The company Web site offers a full rundown of products, information on application tools, and a store locator.*

P.O. Box 2535

Hudson, OH 44236

Phone: 800-321-3444

www.floodco.com

Heritage Vinyl Products *manufactures vinyl deck products.*

661 Anderson Ave.

Pittsburgh, PA 15220

Phone: 800-473-3623

www.heritagevinyl.com

Lindal Cedar Homes *builds cedar homes that can be shipped precut and assembled on your site. The company offers models in a book of plans and a CD-Rom.*

P.O. Box 24426

Seattle, WA 98124

Phone: 800-426-0536

www.lindal.com

Malibu Intermatic Incorporated *offers an impressive assortment of garden and landscape lighting solutions. The Web site presents different lighting scenarios and free literature.*

Intermatic Plaza

Spring Grove, IL 60081-9698

Phone: 815-675-7000

www.intermatic.com

Punch Software *produces deck and landscape design software for the homeowner.*

7900 NW 100th St., Ste. LL6

Kansas City, MO 64153

Phone: 816-891-0025

www.punchsoftware.com

Southern Pine Council *is a nonprofit trade promotion group. Construction details and building tips for southern pine, complete project plans, and other helpful information are all described in a free catalog.*

P.O. Box 641700

Kenner, LA 70064

Phone: 504-443-4464

www.southernpine.com

resource guide

Timber Holdings Ltd. *imports exotic outdoor hardwoods, including ipé and jarrah, under the brand name Iron Wood. The wood offers unique resistance to decay and insects. Call for a free catalog and deck project brochure.*

2400 West Cornell

Milwaukee, WI 53209

Phone: 414-445-8989

www.ironwoods.com

TimberTech Limited *products combine recycled wood and polymers to form complete deck systems that include railings, fascia boards, and a variety of planking. Call for a free catalog.*

P.O. Box 182880

Columbus, OH 43218

Phone: 800-307-7780

www.timbertech.com

Trex Decks *is a leading manufacturer of recycled wood and plastic decking materials. Free literature, a materials guide, and design ideas are available. Complete service and a retailer guide are provided.*

www.trex.com

Western Wood Products Association (WWPA) *develops standards and sets levels of quality for western lumber and products made from western softwood species. Technical information is available via fax or on its Web site.*

522 SW 5th Ave.

Portland, OR 97204-2122

Phone: 503-224-3930/ Fax: 503-224-3934

www.wwpa.org

glossary

Accent lighting Lighting that highlights a space or object to emphasize its character.

Ambient lighting General illumination for an area.

Backlighting Illumination placed behind or to the side of an object. See "Silhouetting."

Balance, in design Equilibrium of the forms in a defined area. Relationships between objects in balance seem natural and comfortable to the eye.

Balusters The vertical pieces, often made of 2x2s or 1x4s, that fill in spaces between rail posts and provide a fencelike structure.

Building codes Municipal rules regulating safe building practices and procedures.

Built-in, deck Any element, such as a bench or planter, that is attached permanently to the deck.

Cantilever Construction that extends beyond its vertical support.

Clearance The amount of space between two fixtures or around furniture. Some clearances may be mandated by codes.

Decay-resistant woods Woods such as redwood, cedar, teak, or mahogany, which are naturally resistant to rot.

Diffused light Indirect or softly-filtered light used for decorative effect.

Fascia Facing that covers the exposed ends and sides of decking to create a finished appearance.

Fire pit A built-in masonry well, typically built into the center of the deck, used to contain a fire.

Floodlights Outdoor lights with strong, bright beams used for security or to highlight an object.

Focal point A design term for the dominant element in a space.

Gazebo A framed structure with a peaked roof that is usually circular or octagonal. A gazebo offers roofed protection from the rain and sun, and can stand alone or be built into the deck.

Grade The ground level. On-grade means at or on the natural ground level.

Harmony, in design A design scheme in which all elements relate pleasingly to one another, forming a complementary and unified whole.

Lattice A cross-pattern structure made of wood, metal, or plastic.

Low-voltage lighting Outdoor lighting fixtures that are powered by low-voltage transformers that convert 120-volt household current to 12 volts.

Path lights Lights that illuminate a path or driveway. Although modular, path lights are typically mounted on portable stakes.

Pergola A framed structure with spaced rafters or a latticework top. Pergolas are favored for decks because they provide light shade while remaining airy.

Pressure-treated lumber Wood that has had preservatives forced into it under pressure to repel rot and insects.

Proportion The relationship of parts or objects to one another based on their size.

Railing cap A horizontal piece of lumber laid flat on top of a post and top rail, covering the end grain of the post.

Rhythm, in design The planned repetition of patterns or motifs.

Scale The size of an object as it relates to the size of people, nearby objects, and the surrounding space.

Silhouetting Lighting an object from behind so that its shape stands in black relief against its background.

Site plan A drawing that maps out a house and yard. Also called a base plan.

Spa, portable Economical, self-contained, aboveground units that run on a standard 120-volt electrical system or on a 240-volt system, depending on size.

Symmetry The identical arrangement of objects or forms on both sides of an imagined or real centerline. Symmetrical arrangements appear formal.

Uplighting A dramatic lighting treatment whereby a light is placed at the base of an object, pointing upwards at it. This is an effective way to highlight trees, plantings, and architectural elements.

index

photo credits

page 1: Bradsimmons.com **page 3:** *all* John Parsekian **page 4:** Brian Vanden Brink **page 6:** Brian Vanden Brink **page 7:** *center* Mark Lohman; *top right* Brian Vanden Brink **page 8:** courtesy of Trex Decks **page 10:** *top* Richard Felber; *bottom* Mark Lohman **page 11:** John Parsekian **page 12:** Brian Vanden Brink, architect: Bernhard and Priestley Architects **page 13:** *top* Brian Vanden Brink, architect: Pete Bethais; *bottom* courtesy of California Redwood Association **page 14:** Mark Lohman **page 15:** John Parsekian **page 16:** Carolyn Bates **page 17:** *top* courtesy of Intermatic/Malibu Lighting; *bottom* courtesy of Trex Decks **page 18:** Brian Vanden Brink **page 19:** *top* Brian Vanden Brink, designer: Weather End Estate Furniture; *bottom* Jessie Walker **page 20:** Phillip H. Ennis Photography, designer: Van Hattum/Simmons **page 21:** *top* John Glover; *bottom* Mark Lohman **page 22:** *top* Brian Vanden Brink, architects: Steven Foote, Perry Dean Rogers, and Partners; *bottom* courtesy of California Redwood Association **page 23:** Brian Vanden Brink, architects: Orcutt Associate Architects **page 24:** Mark Lohman **page 25:** *top* Brian Vanden Brink; *bottom* Walter Chandoha **page 26:** courtesy of the Southern Forest Products Association **page 27:** John Parsekian **page 28:** *top left* courtesy of Arch Wood Protection; *top right* courtesy of DRLA; *bottom* courtesy of Trex Decks **page 29:** Richard Felber **page 30:** John Parsekian **page 31:** courtesy of California Redwood Association **page 32:** Brian Vanden Brink, architects: Horiuchi and Solien Landscape Architects **page 33:** *top* Carolyn Bates; *bottom* Gay Bumgarner/ Positive Images **page 34:** *top* courtesy of Hickson Corporation; *bottom* Brian Vanden Brink, architect: Elliot and Elliot Architects **page 35:** Brian Vanden Brink **page 36:** courtesy of Correct Deck **page 37:** *top* Brian Vanden Brink, designer: Weather End Estate Furniture; *bottom* courtesy of California Redwood Association **page 38:** *top* Anne Gummerson; *bottom* Mark Lohman **page 39:** Brian Vanden Brink, designer: Weather End Estate Furniture **pages 40-41:** *top left* Walter Chandoha; *top right* Jessie Walker; *bottom right* courtesy of Arch Wood Protection; *bottom left* John Glover, designer: Kristina Fitzsimmons **page 42:** Bradsimmons.com **page 43:** courtesy of Timbertech **pages 44-45:** *top left* Tony Giammarino; *top right* Jessie Walker, designer: Ellen Van Buskirk; *bottom right* John Glover, designer: A. Titchmarsh; *bottom left* Carolyn Bates **page 46:** courtesy of Arch Wood Protection; *bottom* courtesy of California Redwood

Association **page 47:** courtesy of Timbertech Limited **page 48:** Jessie Walker, builder: Gregory Onsager **page 50:** *top left* John Parsekian; *top right* courtesy of Trex Decks; *bottom* Carolyn Bates **page 51:** John Parsekian **page 52:** Jessie Walker **page 53:** *top* Jessie Walker; *bottom left* Tony Giammarino; *bottom right* Jerry Howard/ Positive Images **page 54:** Carolyn Bates **page 55:** John Parsekian **page 56:** *top* Carolyn Bates; *bottom* courtesy of Elyria Fence Company **page 57:** courtesy of California Redwood Association **page 58:** Tony Giammarino **page 59:** *top left* John W. Mayo/ Unicorn Stock Photos; *top right* James M. Mejuto; *bottom right* courtesy of the Southern Forest Products Association; *bottom left* Carolyn Bates **page 60:** *top and bottom* John Parsekian **page 61:** *top* Walter Chandoha; *bottom* courtesy of Trex Decks **page 62:** Jessie Walker **page 63:** *top* courtesy of the Southern Forest Products Association; *bottom* Gay Bumgarner/ Positive Images **page 64:** courtesy of Arch Wood Protection **page 65:** *top* Jessie Walker; *center* Liz Ball/Positive Images; *bottom* Gay Bumgarner/Positive Images **page 66:** *left* Brian Vanden Brink, architect: Rob Whitten **page 67:** *center* courtesy of Trex Decks; *top right* Brian Vanden Brink, architects: Donham and Sweeney; *bottom right* Brian Vanden Brink, architect: John Morris **page 68:** *top left and top right* Brian Vanden Brink, top left architect: John Morris, top right architects: Steven Foote, Perry Dean Rogers, and Partners; *bottom* Phillip H. Ennis Photography, designer: Four Seasons Greenhouses **page 69:** Brian Vanden Brink, architect: Jeremiah Eck **page 70:** courtesy of California Redwood Association **page 71:** *top* Brian Vanden Brink, architect: Stephen Blatt; *bottom* Phillip H. Ennis Photography, architect: Mojo Stumer **page 72:** Melabee M Miller, builder: Doyle Builders **page 74:** *top* Michael Thompson, designer: Sarah Robertson; *bottom* Jessie Walker **page 75:** *top* K. Rice/ H. Armstrong Roberts **page 76:** courtesy of the California Redwood Association **page 77:** *top* Brian Vanden Brink, architect: John Silverio; *bottom left* Brian Vanden Brink, architect: Sam Van Dam; *bottom right* Jessie Walker **page 78:** *top* Jessie Walker; *bottom* Brian Vanden Brink, architect: Elliot and Elliot **page 79:** Jessie Walker **page 80:** *top* Tony Giammarino; *center* Gay Bumgarner/ Positive Images; *bottom* Tony Giammarino **page 81:** courtesy of Thompson's Water Seal **page 82:** Jessie Walker **page 83:** *top* H. Armstrong Roberts; *center* Ann Reilly/ Positive Images; *bottom* Gay Bumgarner/ Positive

Images **page 84:** John Parsekian; *bottom* Unicorn Stock Photos **page 85:** John Parsekian **page 86:** Jessie Walker **page 87:** *top* Tony Giammarino; *bottom* Brian Vanden Brink **page 88:** Brian Vanden Brink, builder: Bullock and Company **page 90:** *top* Ann Reilly/ Positive Images; *bottom left and right* John Parsekian **page 91:** Bradsimmons.com **page 92:** *top* Brian Vanden Brink; *bottom* James M. Mejuto **page 93:** *top left* James M. Mejuto; *bottom right* Jessie Walker **pages 94-95:** Bradsimmons.com **page 96-97:** *top center* Brian Vanden Brink; *bottom right* courtesy of the California Redwood Association; *bottom left* Brian Vanden Brink, architect: Royal Barry Wills **page 98:** *top* Bradsimmons.com; *bottom right* Mark Lohman; *bottom left* Ann Reilly/ Positive Images **page 99:** Bradsimmons.com **pages 100-101:** *left* courtesy of Wolman Lumber; *top right* Walter Chandoha; *bottom right and center* Bradsimmons.com **page 102:** courtesy of Trex Decks **page 104:** *top left* courtesy of Lindal Cedar Homes; *bottom* Eurostock: K.Rice/H. Armstrong Roberts **page 105:** Brian Vanden Brink **page 106:** *top left* courtesy of Western Cedar Association; *bottom right* Brian Vanden Brink **page 107:** John Parsekian **page 108:** *top* courtesy of Ernest Braun/California Redwood Association; *bottom* Walter Chandoha **page 109:** Anne Gummerson Photography **page 110:** *top left* Brian Vanden Brink; *bottom right* James Housel; *bottom left* Jessie Walker **page 111:** Brian Vanden Brink **page 112:** Bradsimmons.com **page 114:** *top* Bradsimmons.com; *bottom left* Tony Giammarino **page 115:** courtesy of California Redwood Association **page 116:** John Parsekian **page 117:** *top* John Glover; *center* courtesy of California Redwood Association; *bottom* Raven Bussolini/Positive Images **page 118:** Brian Vanden Brink **page 119:** *top* Michael Thompson; *bottom* Melabee M Miller **page 120:** Bradsimmons.com **page 121:** *top* Phillip H. Ennis Photography; *bottom* Anne Gummerson **page 122:** courtesy of Arch Wood Protection **pages 123 and 124:** courtesy of Trex Decks

Have a home improvement, decorating, or gardening project? Look for these and other fine
Creative Homeowner books wherever books are sold.

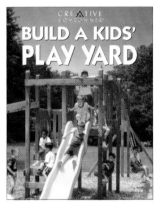

Build, step by step, the play structures kids love. 200+ color photos, drawings. 144 pp., 8½"×10⅞"
BOOK #: 277662

Step-by-step deck building for the novice. 500+ color photos, illustrations. 192 pp.; 8½"×10⅞"
BOOK #: 277162

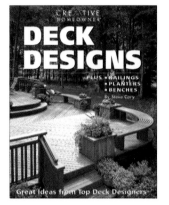

Plans from top deck designer-builders. 300+ color photos, illustrations. 192 pp.; 8½"×10⅞"
BOOK #: 277369

Design ideas, planning advice, and projects. 460+ color photos, illustrations. 160 pp; 8½"×10⅞"
BOOK #: 274804

How to build 20 furniture projects. 470+ color photos, illustrations. 208 pp.; 8½"×10⅞"
BOOK #: 277462

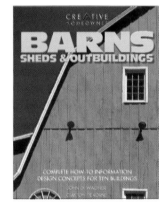

Plan, construct, and finish outbuildings. 600+ color photos, illustrations. 208 pp.; 8½"×10⅞"
BOOK #: 277818

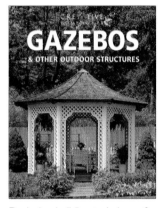

Designing, building techniques for yard structures. 450+ color photos, illustrations. 160 pp.; 8½"×10⅞"
BOOK #: 277138

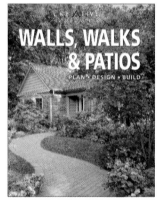

Build landscape structures from concrete, brick, stone. 370+ color illustrations. 192 pp.; 8½"×10⅞"
BOOK #: 277994

Newest designs, products. 200+ color photos. 128 pp.; 8½"×10⅞"
BOOK #: 277183

Idyllic at-home getaways. 200+ color photos. 128 pp.; 8½"×10⅞"
BOOK #: 279456

Impressive guide to garden design and plant selection. 600+ color photos, illustrations. 320 pp.; 9"×10"
BOOK #: 274615

Lavishly illustrated with portraits of over 100 flowering plants; 500+ color photos. 208 pp.; 9"×10"
BOOK #: 274032

For more information, and to order direct, call 800-631-7795; in New Jersey 201-934-7100.
www.creativehomeowner.com